Table of Contents

Introduction

Embarking on the journey of starting a food truck and mobile catering business can be both thrilling and fulfilling, especially for those who have a deep passion for food and a desire to provide exceptional service. Imagine combining your culinary skills with the freedom to move and serve customers in different locations it's a unique business model that's full of potential. This comprehensive guide is here to walk you through all the crucial steps and considerations to ensure your food truck and mobile catering business thrives from the start and continues to grow successfully.

In the pages ahead, we'll cover everything you need to know. We'll start by helping you assess your skills and resources essentially, taking a good, hard look at what you bring to the table and what you might need to acquire or improve. Understanding your target market is another critical piece of the puzzle. Who are your potential customers? What are their tastes and preferences? Answering these questions will guide your menu creation and marketing efforts.

A solid business plan is the backbone of any successful venture. We'll guide you through developing a plan that outlines your business goals, strategies, and financial projections. Alongside this, navigating the legal and regulatory requirements can be daunting, but it's necessary to ensure your business operates smoothly and legally. We'll provide clear, step-by-step instructions to help you set up your mobile kitchen, adhering to all health and safety regulations.

Building a strong brand and online presence is paramount in today's digital age. Your brand is your business's identity, it's what sets you apart from competitors and creates a loyal customer base. We'll explore strategies for creating a compelling brand and leveraging social media and other online platforms to attract and engage customers.

Acquiring customers and securing events are the lifeblood of your business. We'll share proven tactics for marketing your food truck and mobile catering services, from attending local events to partnering with other businesses. Exceptional service is not just a goal but a necessity. Positive customer experiences and word-of-mouth referrals can make or break your business, so we'll emphasize the importance of top-notch customer service.

Finally, growing your food truck and mobile catering business involves expanding your menu offerings and exploring new markets. We'll discuss ways to innovate and diversify, ensuring your business remains fresh and appealing to both existing and new customers.

Whether you're a seasoned entrepreneur or just starting out, this guide is packed with valuable insights and practical advice to help you navigate the challenges and seize the opportunities in the food truck and mobile catering industry. So, let's dive in and discover everything you need to know to start and grow a successful food truck and mobile catering business.

Chapter 1: Introduction to the Food Truck and Mobile Catering Business

Starting a food truck and mobile catering business is an exciting and rewarding adventure. With the growing popularity of food trucks and the increasing demand for mobile catering services, this industry offers a unique chance for entrepreneurs to showcase their culinary talents and reach a diverse range of customers. In this chapter, we will dive into the essentials of the food truck and mobile catering business. We'll explore what these businesses are all about, their advantages and challenges, and why you should consider venturing into this dynamic industry.

What is a Food Truck and Mobile Catering Business?

Imagine a food truck as a mobile kitchen on wheels, bustling with activity and tantalizing aromas. These trucks are equipped with all the necessary equipment and appliances to cook and serve food right on the spot. They bring the kitchen directly to the customers, whether they're parked outside office complexes, at festivals, in parks, or even at weddings.

On the other hand, mobile catering businesses offer a broader range of services. They often cater to events and private parties, providing customized menus and serving larger groups of people. Mobile caterers bring the restaurant experience to the customer, wherever that may be. Both food trucks and mobile catering businesses offer convenient and flexible dining options, allowing entrepreneurs to adapt to changing customer demands and explore new markets.

Advantages and Challenges

Running a food truck or mobile catering business comes with several advantages. First and foremost, it requires a lower initial investment compared to setting up a traditional brick-and-mortar restaurant. This makes it a more accessible option for many aspiring entrepreneurs. The mobility aspect is another significant benefit, as it enables business owners to reach a larger customer base and participate in various events and festivals. You can take your culinary creations to where the crowds are, maximizing exposure and sales opportunities.

Additionally, the food truck and mobile catering industry provide a platform for culinary creativity and innovation. Entrepreneurs can experiment with different cuisines and menu items to cater to a wide range of tastes and preferences. This flexibility allows for a unique and diverse culinary experience for customers, keeping them coming back for more.

However, like any business, there are challenges to consider. Weather can be unpredictable, affecting outdoor events and sales. Limited storage and kitchen space on the truck can be a constraint, requiring efficient planning and organization. Compliance with local regulations and obtaining the necessary permits can also be a hurdle, but with proper preparation, these challenges can be managed effectively.

Why Start a Food Truck or Mobile Catering Business?

So, why should you consider starting a food truck or mobile catering business? There are plenty of compelling reasons. Firstly, it offers a more affordable entry point into the food industry compared to opening a traditional restaurant. This makes it an attractive option for aspiring chefs and culinary enthusiasts who want to showcase their skills without the hefty investment.

Moreover, the demand for on-the-go dining experiences continues to grow. People are always on the lookout for convenient, high-quality food options, and food trucks and mobile caterers are perfectly positioned to meet this need. With the right marketing strategies, you can attract a loyal customer base and establish your brand in the industry.

The mobility aspect of these businesses also opens up a world of opportunities. You can participate in local events, festivals, and even cater to corporate or private functions. This variety in clientele and venues adds excitement and diversity to your business, ensuring that no two days are the same.

In the upcoming chapters, we will delve deeper into the various aspects of starting and growing a food truck and mobile catering business. We'll discuss how to assess your skills and resources, understand your target market, develop a solid business plan, and navigate the legal and regulatory considerations.

So, if you are passionate about food, enjoy interacting with customers, and have a knack for culinary creativity, the food truck and mobile catering industry might be the perfect fit for your entrepreneurial dreams. Let's dive in and explore the wonderful world of food trucks and mobile catering!

Chapter 2: Assessing Your Skills and Resources

Starting a food truck and mobile catering business is an exciting journey, but before you hit the road, it's vital to take a step back and assess your skills and resources. This initial evaluation will help you understand your strengths and pinpoint areas that may need improvement. By doing so, you'll be better equipped to make informed decisions and set realistic goals, ensuring a smoother path to success.

Evaluating Your Skills

First things first: let's talk about your skills. It's not just about knowing how to cook, although that's a significant part of it. Running a food truck and mobile catering business requires a blend of culinary talent, business acumen, and excellent customer service. Here are some questions to guide you:

Culinary Skills:

- Do you have a genuine passion for cooking? Are you familiar with various cuisines and capable of creating delicious, innovative menus that will captivate your target market?

- If your culinary skills aren't up to par, are you open to learning? Alternatively, would you consider hiring a chef to help you?

Business Acumen:

- Running a food truck isn't just about the food. Do you understand pricing, budgeting, and inventory management? Can you handle the business side of things?
- If you're not confident in your business skills, are you willing to take courses or partner with someone who has this expertise?

Customer Service:

- How comfortable are you with interacting with customers? Providing exceptional service is crucial for success in this industry.
- If customer service isn't your strong suit, consider seeking training or hiring staff who excel in this area.

Assessing Your Resources

Now, let's shift gears and talk about resources. Understanding what you have and what you need is key to starting and growing your business. Consider these aspects:

Financial Resources:

- Do you have enough funds to get your business off the ground? Think about the costs involved in purchasing or leasing a food truck, obtaining necessary permits and licenses, buying equipment and ingredients, and covering initial operating expenses.

- If your funds are limited, look into financing options or start small and gradually expand.

Equipment and Supplies:

- Take stock of the equipment you already have. Does it meet the requirements for a food truck or mobile kitchen?
- Consider the need for cooking equipment, refrigeration, storage, and utensils. Identify any gaps and make a list of the additional equipment you'll need.

Network and Connections:

- Evaluate your network within the food and hospitality industry. Do you have suppliers who can offer high-quality ingredients at competitive prices?
- Can you connect with event organizers or other food truck owners for guidance and support? A strong network can be incredibly beneficial.

Time Commitment:

- Reflect on your available time and lifestyle commitments. Running a food truck and mobile catering business demands a significant time investment, especially during peak operating hours and catering events.

- Make sure you're ready to dedicate the necessary time and energy to make your business a success.

Conclusion

Assessing your skills and resources is a critical step in launching your food truck and mobile catering business. This thorough evaluation will help you identify areas for improvement and ensure you have the necessary resources. By understanding your strengths and weaknesses, you can plan effectively and allocate your finances, equipment, and time wisely. Use this chapter as a guide to reflect on your current situation and make the necessary adjustments to set yourself up for success in this exciting industry.

Chapter 3: Understanding Your Target Market

Understanding your target market is a pivotal step in launching and growing your food truck and mobile catering business. When you pinpoint and comprehend who your ideal customers are, you can customize your menu, marketing strategies, and overall business approach to cater effectively to their needs and preferences.

Identifying Your Target Market

To identify your target market, let's break down a few critical factors:

Demographics

Demographic information includes details like age, gender, income level, occupation, and location. This data is invaluable because it helps you figure out who your potential customers are and what their specific preferences and needs might be. For example, if your food truck is parked near a university campus, your primary target market may consist of students looking for quick and affordable meal options. Understanding the demographics of your area allows you to tailor your offerings to meet these specific needs.

Psychographics

Psychographics delve into the attitudes, values, interests, and lifestyle choices of your target market. This information goes beyond surface-level data, providing insights into what motivates your customers and how you can appeal to their preferences. For instance, if your target market includes health-conscious individuals, focusing on organic and nutritious food options can make your business stand out. Knowing what drives your customers' choices allows you to align your business with their values.

Preferences and Behaviors

Analyzing your target market's preferences and behaviors helps you understand the types of food they enjoy, their dining habits, and their willingness to try new cuisines. Gathering this information can be done through surveys, social media interactions, or customer feedback. This knowledge enables you to tailor your menu and offerings to attract and retain customers. For example, if your customers are adventurous eaters, introducing unique, seasonal dishes might keep them coming back for more.

Conducting Market Research

Once you've identified your target market, conducting thorough market research is essential to gather additional insights and validate your assumptions. Here are some methods to consider:

Online Research

Utilize online resources like social media platforms, online forums, and industry publications to gather information about your target market. By analyzing their conversations, preferences, and behaviors, you gain a deeper understanding of their needs and wants. Social media, in particular, is a goldmine for observing trends and getting real-time feedback.

Competitor Analysis

Studying your competitors who cater to a similar target market can provide valuable insights. Analyze their menu offerings, pricing strategies, and marketing tactics. This will help you identify gaps or opportunities in the market that you can capitalize on. For example, if you notice a competitor's menu lacks vegetarian options and you have a significant vegetarian demographic, you could fill that niche.

Surveys and Focus Groups

Conducting surveys or organizing focus groups allows you to gather direct feedback from your target market. This provides invaluable insights into their preferences, expectations, and satisfaction levels. Use this information to refine your offerings and enhance the customer experience. For instance, if customers express a desire for faster service, you might streamline your ordering process.

Applying Customer Insights

After gathering insights about your target market, it's crucial to apply this knowledge to every aspect of your business. Here are some key areas to focus on:

Menu Development

Tailor your menu to reflect the preferences and dietary requirements of your target market. Consider offering a variety of options that cater to different tastes and preferences. If your target market includes families, for example, including kid-friendly options could be beneficial.

Pricing Strategy

Determine pricing strategies that align with your target market's willingness to pay. Consider factors such as value for money and affordability. If your market consists largely of budget-conscious college students, offering combo deals or loyalty discounts might be effective.

Marketing and Advertising

Craft your marketing messages and promotional activities to resonate with your target market. Utilize social media platforms, targeted online advertising, and local community outreach to reach potential customers. For instance, if your audience is tech-savvy, investing in a robust online presence and engaging content could be particularly effective.

Customer Experience

Ensure that every interaction with your customers reflects their preferences and expectations. Provide exceptional service, personalized recommendations, and a welcoming atmosphere to build loyalty and positive word-of-mouth. For example, remembering regular customers' names and orders can make them feel valued and appreciated.

Conclusion

Understanding your target market is essential for the success of your food truck and mobile catering business. By identifying and analyzing their preferences, behaviors, and needs, you can tailor your offerings and business strategies to meet their expectations. Conducting market research and applying customer insights will give you a competitive edge and help you build a loyal customer base. Stay tuned for the next chapter, where we will delve into developing your business plan.

Chapter 4: Developing Your Business Plan

Creating a comprehensive business plan is one of the most crucial steps in starting and growing your food truck and mobile catering business. Think of it as your blueprint for success a detailed guide that helps you achieve your goals and navigate the inevitable challenges along the way.

What is a Business Plan?

A business plan is a detailed document outlining your business goals and the strategies you will use to achieve them. It acts as a roadmap for your food truck and mobile catering business, helping you make informed decisions and attract potential investors or lenders. A comprehensive business plan typically includes the following sections:

1. **Executive Summary:** This is a snapshot of your business, summarizing key points from each section of the plan. It should be concise, compelling, and designed to grab the reader's attention right away.

2. **Company Description:** Here, you'll describe your food truck or mobile catering business in detail, including its legal structure, location, and any unique selling

points or competitive advantages that set you apart from the competition.

3. **Market Analysis:** Conduct a thorough analysis of your target market. This includes understanding the demographics, psychographics, preferences, and behaviors of your potential customers. Identify who they are and highlight the market trends and opportunities that support your business idea.

4. **Products and Services:** Provide a detailed description of the food and services you plan to offer. Include information about your menu, pricing strategy, and any additional services you might provide, such as catering for events or private parties.

5. **Marketing and Sales Strategies:** Outline how you plan to attract and retain customers. This should include details on branding, advertising, social media presence, and customer acquisition tactics. Think about how you'll differentiate your business from competitors and build a loyal customer base.

6. **Organization and Management:** Describe the organizational structure of your business and the roles and responsibilities of key team members. Highlight any relevant industry experience or expertise that you or your team members bring to the business.

7. **Financial Projections:** Develop financial forecasts, including income statements, cash flow statements, and balance sheets. Project your revenue and expenses for the first three to five years,

taking into account startup costs, operational expenses, and potential growth opportunities. This section is crucial for showing investors and lenders that you understand your business's financial viability.

8. **Funding Request:** If you need financing, this section should detail your funding requirements and how the funds will be used. Be specific about the amount of funding needed, the purpose of the funds, and your repayment plan.

9. **Appendix:** Include any supporting documents, such as permits, licenses, leases, or market research data, in this section.

Why is a Business Plan Important?

A business plan is essential for several reasons:

1. **Strategic Planning:** Developing a business plan forces you to think critically about your goals, strategies, and the steps required to achieve them. It helps you identify potential roadblocks and develop contingency plans.

2. **Attracting Funding:** Investors and lenders will often require a business plan to assess the viability of your food truck or mobile catering business. A well-prepared business plan demonstrates your understanding of the industry, market, and financial projections, increasing your chances of securing funding.

3. **Focus and Organization:** A business plan provides structure and clarity, keeping you focused on your goals and ensuring all aspects of your business are properly considered. It serves as a reference document to track progress and make adjustments as needed.

4. **Communication:** A comprehensive business plan enables effective communication with stakeholders, employees, and potential partners or customers. It conveys your vision and the value proposition of your food truck or mobile catering business.

Conclusion

Developing a business plan is a critical step in starting and growing your food truck and mobile catering business. It serves as your roadmap for success, guiding your decision-making processes and increasing your chances of attracting funding and achieving your goals. Take the time to thoroughly research and develop a comprehensive business plan that reflects the unique aspects of your business and positions you for success in the industry.

By carefully crafting and following your business plan, you'll be well-equipped to turn your culinary dreams into a thriving reality. So, roll up your sleeves, dive into the details, and set the stage for your food truck and mobile catering venture to flourish!

Chapter 5: Legal and Regulatory Considerations

When you're setting out to start your food truck or mobile catering business, navigating the legal and regulatory landscape is crucial. Understanding the rules that govern this industry will help you operate smoothly and avoid any legal pitfalls. In this chapter, we'll dive into the key legal and regulatory considerations you need to be aware of to ensure your business is compliant and set up for success.

Understanding Local Laws and Permits

First things first, you need to familiarize yourself with the local laws and regulations that apply to food service establishments. These laws can vary significantly from one place to another, so it's important to do your homework. Here are some key areas to focus on:

Business Licenses and Permits:

- To legally operate your food truck or mobile catering business, you will need to obtain various licenses and permits. This might include a general business license, a food service permit, and a mobile food vendor permit.
- The specifics can vary, so check with your local health department or regulatory agency to find out exactly what you need.

Zoning Regulations:

- Zoning regulations will dictate where you can park and operate your food truck. Some areas have restrictions, like prohibiting food trucks near residential areas or schools.
- Make sure you understand and comply with these regulations to avoid any legal trouble down the line.

Food Safety and Handling:

- Food safety is paramount. You must adhere to strict guidelines for food storage, preparation, and handling to ensure your customers' health and safety.
- This typically involves obtaining a food handler's permit and following proper sanitation practices.

Insurance Coverage:

- Adequate insurance coverage is crucial. Consider getting general liability insurance, which covers bodily injury and property damage, and product liability insurance to protect against claims related to the food you serve.

Employment Laws:

- If you plan to hire employees, familiarize yourself with employment laws. These laws cover areas like minimum wage, overtime pay, meal and rest breaks, and workplace safety.

- Compliance is essential to avoid legal issues and to ensure a fair and safe working environment for your team.

Tax Obligations:

- As a business owner, you have certain tax obligations. This might include obtaining an Employer Identification Number (EIN), filing quarterly taxes, keeping detailed financial records, and complying with sales tax requirements.
- Consult with a tax professional or accountant to make sure you're meeting all your tax obligations.

Intellectual Property Considerations:

- When developing your brand and logo, it's important to consider intellectual property rights. Conduct a thorough search to ensure that your business name, logo, and branding elements don't infringe on any existing trademarks or copyrights.
- Consulting with an intellectual property attorney can guide you through this process and help protect your intellectual property rights.

Conclusion

Understanding and complying with the legal and regulatory requirements of the food truck and mobile catering industry is critical for the success and longevity of your business. Take the time to research and understand the specific laws and regulations in your area. Don't hesitate to consult with professionals whether they're lawyers, accountants, or industry experts when necessary. By operating within the bounds of the law, you can focus on what you do best: providing exceptional food and service to your customers without the worry of potential legal issues.

Chapter 6: Setting Up Your Mobile Kitchen

Setting up your mobile kitchen is one of the most critical steps in starting your food truck or mobile catering business. Think of your mobile kitchen as the heart of your operation it's where all the magic happens, where you prepare those mouth-watering meals, and where you provide exceptional service to your customers. In this chapter, we'll dive into the key considerations and steps involved in creating a functional, efficient, and compliant mobile kitchen.

Designing Your Mobile Kitchen

The first step in setting up your mobile kitchen is designing the layout and figuring out the equipment and supplies you'll need. This will largely depend on the type of cuisine you plan to serve and the size of your truck or catering unit. Here are some important considerations:

1. **Space Optimization:** Given the limited space in a mobile kitchen, it's crucial to make the most of every inch. Strategically place equipment, workstations, and storage areas to maximize functionality and allow your staff to move easily. A well-thought-out layout ensures smooth operations and efficient workflow.

2. **Equipment Selection:** Choose the right equipment that suits your menu and cooking style. This might include grills, fryers, ovens, refrigerators, sinks, and

storage units. Opt for high-quality, durable, and energy-efficient equipment that can withstand the demands of a mobile kitchen. Remember, the reliability of your equipment is key to maintaining service quality.

3. **Ventilation and Exhaust Systems:** Proper ventilation is essential to maintain air quality and remove cooking odors. This is important not only for the comfort and well-being of your staff but also to comply with health regulations. Ensure you have a robust ventilation and exhaust system installed.

4. **Fire Safety Measures:** Safety should always be a priority. Install fire suppression systems and keep portable fire extinguishers on hand to prevent and extinguish potential kitchen fires. Compliance with local fire safety codes and regulations is not just a legal requirement but a necessary step to protect your business and staff.

Procuring Equipment and Supplies

Once you have a solid design for your mobile kitchen, the next step is procuring the necessary equipment and supplies. Here's how to go about it:

1. **Research Suppliers:** Look for reputable suppliers who specialize in commercial kitchen equipment and supplies. Compare prices, warranties, and customer reviews to ensure you're making informed purchasing decisions. Reliable

suppliers can make a big difference in the quality and longevity of your equipment.

2. **Budget Considerations:** Determine your budget for equipment and supplies and prioritize essential items. Depending on your budget constraints, you might consider buying new or used equipment. However, if you choose used equipment, make sure it's in good working condition to avoid frequent repairs.

3. **Safety and Quality:** Prioritize safety and quality when selecting equipment and supplies. Ensure all equipment meets safety standards and that supplies, such as utensils and storage containers, are food-grade and durable. This not only ensures compliance but also enhances the overall efficiency and safety of your operations.

4. **Stock Up on Essentials:** Beyond cooking equipment, remember to stock up on essential items like cleaning supplies, food packaging materials, cooking utensils, and disposable plates and cutlery. Think of everything you'll need to serve your food efficiently and maintain a clean and organized workspace.

Storage and Organization

Efficient storage and organization are key to a successful mobile kitchen. Here are some tips to keep your space tidy and functional:

1. **Utilize Vertical Space:** Install shelves, hooks, and racks to maximize your storage capacity. Using vertical space helps keep your workspace clutter-free and allows easy access to items, which is vital in a compact mobile kitchen.

2. **Organize Based on Frequency of Use:** Arrange your equipment, utensils, and supplies based on how often you use them. Keep frequently used items within easy reach, and store less frequently used items in areas that are accessible but out of the way.

3. **Maintain Cleanliness and Sanitation:** Regularly clean and sanitize your storage areas to prevent cross-contamination and maintain food safety standards. Develop an organized system for rotating perishable items to prevent food spoilage.

Sourcing Ingredients

Your ingredients are the foundation of your culinary creations. Here are some strategies for sourcing fresh and high-quality ingredients:

1. **Local Suppliers:** Establish relationships with local farmers, fishermen, and food suppliers who can provide you with fresh and seasonal ingredients. Supporting local businesses not only ensures high-quality ingredients but also promotes sustainability.

2. **Farmers' Markets:** Consider sourcing ingredients from farmers' markets, where

you can find a wide variety of fresh produce, dairy, meat, and specialty products. Engaging with vendors helps build strong connections and negotiate favorable purchasing terms.

3. **Online Suppliers:** Explore online platforms that connect chefs with local and specialty food producers. These platforms offer a convenient way to source unique ingredients and support small-scale food producers.

4. **Sustainable Practices:** Embrace sustainable sourcing practices, such as using locally sourced and organic ingredients whenever possible. This not only has a positive environmental impact but also attracts customers who value sustainable food practices.

Conclusion

Setting up your mobile kitchen requires careful planning and attention to detail in terms of layout, equipment, supplies, storage, and sourcing. A well-designed and well-equipped mobile kitchen will enable you to efficiently serve delicious meals to your customers while maintaining cleanliness, compliance with food safety regulations, and an organized workspace. In the next chapter, we'll discuss the importance of building your brand and online presence in the food truck and mobile catering industry. Keep up the great work, and let's continue this journey towards creating a successful food truck business!

Chapter 7: Building Your Brand and Online Presence

In today's digital age, building a strong brand and online presence is essential for the success of any business, including food trucks and mobile catering businesses. Your brand is what sets you apart from your competitors and allows you to connect with your target market. Your online presence enables you to reach a wider audience, engage with potential customers, and build credibility and trust. In this chapter, we will explore strategies for building your brand and establishing a robust online presence.

Defining Your Brand Identity

Before you can start building your brand, you need to define your brand identity. This involves identifying your unique selling propositions, your target market, and your brand values.

1. **Unique Selling Propositions (USPs):** These are the qualities or attributes that make your food truck or catering business stand out. It could be your signature dishes, your commitment to using locally sourced ingredients, or your exceptional customer service. Reflect on what makes your business special and how you want to be perceived.

2. **Target Market:** Consider the demographics, psychographics, preferences, and behaviors of your potential customers. Are they young professionals, families, or food enthusiasts? Understanding your audience helps tailor your branding and marketing efforts to appeal to them effectively.

3. **Brand Values:** These are the principles and beliefs that guide your business decisions and actions. It could be a commitment to sustainability, supporting local farmers, or providing healthy and delicious food options. Your brand values should resonate with the values of your target market to create a strong connection.

Designing Your Visual Identity

Your visual identity plays a crucial role in building brand recognition and differentiation. It includes your logo, color palette, typography, and overall visual style.

1. **Logo:** Start by creating a distinctive logo that reflects your brand's personality and values. It should be memorable, versatile, and easily recognizable. Consider hiring a professional graphic designer to create a logo that captures the essence of your brand.

2. **Color Palette:** Establish a consistent color palette that reflects your brand's identity. Colors evoke specific emotions and associations, so choose ones that align with

your target market and the tone of your business. Use these colors consistently across all your branding materials, including your website, signage, and social media profiles.

3. **Typography:** Choose fonts that are legible and appropriate for your brand's personality. Consider using different fonts for headings, subheadings, and body text to create hierarchy and visual interest.

Creating Your Online Presence

Having a strong online presence is crucial for attracting and engaging customers. Here's how to get started:

1. **Professional Website:** Create a professional website that showcases your brand, menu, and contact information. Your website should be visually appealing, easy to navigate, and optimized for mobile devices. Include high-quality photos of your food and a user-friendly menu that clearly lists your offerings and prices.

2. **Social Media Platforms:** Establish a presence on social media platforms that are popular among your target market, such as Facebook, Instagram, Twitter, or TikTok. Regularly update your social media profiles with engaging content, including mouth-watering food photos, behind-the-scenes glimpses, and promotions or special offers. Interact with

your followers by responding to comments and messages promptly.

3. **Content Creation:** Consider starting a blog or YouTube channel to share your culinary expertise, recipes, and stories. This can help establish you as an authority in the industry and attract a loyal following.

Engaging with Your Customers

Building a strong brand and online presence is not just about advertising and promotion. It's also about building relationships with your customers and creating a positive and memorable experience.

1. **Customer Interaction:** Engage with your customers both online and offline. Respond to customer reviews and feedback on platforms like Yelp, Google My Business, and social media. Address any concerns or issues promptly and professionally. This shows that you value your customers' opinions and are committed to providing exceptional service.

2. **Promotions and Contests:** Organize contests, giveaways, or collaborations with other local businesses to create buzz and engage your customers. Encourage your customers to share their experiences on social media by creating Instagrammable moments or offering incentives for user-generated content.

Monitoring and Analyzing Your Online Presence

Finally, it's important to constantly monitor and analyze your online presence to ensure that your branding and marketing efforts are effective.

1. **Analytics Tools:** Use analytics tools to track website traffic, social media engagement, and customer interactions. This data will provide valuable insights into what's working and what's not.

2. **Adjust Strategies:** Adjust your strategies based on the insights you gain from these metrics to continuously improve and optimize your online presence. Being flexible and responsive to your audience's needs and behaviors will help you stay relevant and successful.

Conclusion

Building a strong brand and online presence is a vital component of starting and growing a successful food truck and mobile catering business. It allows you to connect with your target market, stand out from your competitors, and create a positive and memorable experience for your customers. By defining your brand identity, designing a compelling visual identity, creating a professional website, and engaging with customers online, you can establish a strong brand and online presence that drives the success of your business.

Invest the time and effort to develop these aspects thoughtfully, and you'll see your business thrive in the competitive world of food trucks and mobile catering.

Chapter 8: Acquiring Customers and Events

One of the most critical aspects of running a successful food truck and mobile catering business is acquiring new customers and securing events. In this chapter, we'll delve into effective strategies and techniques to help you attract customers and secure those all-important events.

1. Create a Marketing Strategy

Let's start with the foundation: a solid marketing strategy. Knowing who your ideal customers are is the first step. Take the time to understand their preferences, behaviors, and what makes them tick. Are they health-conscious? Do they crave unique, gourmet experiences? Once you have a clear picture, you can tailor your marketing efforts to resonate with them.

Next, craft a compelling brand message that highlights what sets your food truck or catering business apart. Maybe it's your signature dishes, the high-quality ingredients you use, or your exceptional personalized service. Use this message consistently across all your marketing channels to build strong brand recognition and loyalty.

2. Utilize Social Media Marketing

In today's digital age, social media platforms are powerful tools for promoting your food truck or catering business. Create accounts on popular platforms like Facebook, Instagram, and Twitter. Regularly post engaging content such as mouth-watering food photos, behind-the-scenes glimpses, and special promotions.

Interact with your followers by promptly responding to comments and messages. Encourage them to share their experiences and pictures of your food on their social media profiles. Consider running contests or giveaways to incentivize user-generated content. This not only increases your exposure but also attracts new customers who are eager to try your offerings.

3. Collaborate with Influencers and Food Bloggers

Influencers and food bloggers can be game-changers for your business. They have a loyal following and can significantly boost your visibility and credibility. Reach out to local influencers and bloggers whose values align with your brand and target market. Offer them a complimentary meal or catering service in exchange for a review or social media promotion.

Make sure their audience matches your target market. A well-placed endorsement from a trusted influencer can create a buzz around your business and attract a surge of new customers.

4. Participate in Food Festivals and Events

Food festivals and events are golden opportunities to showcase your culinary skills and attract a broader audience. Research local food festivals, street fairs, and community events where you can set up your food truck or offer catering services. Contact event organizers well in advance to secure your spot and understand their requirements.

Consider offering special menus or exclusive dishes for these events to entice attendees. Engage with customers at the event, provide exceptional service, and distribute promotional materials like business cards or flyers to encourage repeat business.

5. Build Relationships with Local Businesses

Networking with local businesses can open doors to lucrative catering opportunities. Reach out to nearby offices, event venues, schools, and community centers to offer your catering services for their meetings, parties, or gatherings. Provide sample menus, testimonials, and references to showcase your capabilities and professionalism.

Consider offering special discounts or packages for corporate clients or exclusive partnerships with event venues. Building strong relationships with local businesses will ensure a steady stream of catering orders and increase your credibility in the industry.

6. Word-of-Mouth Referrals

Never underestimate the power of word-of-mouth referrals. Encourage your satisfied customers to spread the word about your food truck or catering business. Offer referral incentives such as discounts or freebies for customers who refer new clients to you.

To enhance the customer experience, provide exceptional service and go the extra mile to exceed their expectations. Consistently deliver delicious food, create a welcoming atmosphere, and provide personalized recommendations. This will help you build a loyal customer base who will happily refer you to others.

7. Online Booking Platforms

Utilize online booking platforms specific to the food truck and catering industry to expand your customer base. These platforms allow customers to easily find and book their favorite food trucks or catering services for events. Sign up for these platforms and optimize your listing with attractive food photos, menu options, pricing, and customer reviews.

By leveraging online booking platforms, you can tap into a wider audience and secure more catering events with ease.

Conclusion

Acquiring customers and securing events is vital for the ongoing success and growth of your food truck or mobile catering business. A well-thought-out marketing strategy, effective use of social media, collaborations with influencers and bloggers, participation in food festivals, building relationships with local businesses, encouraging word-of-mouth referrals, and utilizing online booking platforms are all strategies that can help you thrive in the competitive food industry. Implement these strategies consistently and adapt them to the evolving needs of your target market to ensure your business continues to grow and succeed.

Chapter 9: Providing Exceptional Service

Providing exceptional service is the cornerstone of a successful food truck and mobile catering business. It's not just about serving delicious food; it's about creating a memorable experience that keeps customers coming back and spreading the word. In this chapter, we will explore strategies and tips to help you deliver outstanding service to your customers, ensuring satisfaction, loyalty, and positive word-of-mouth referrals.

Understanding Customer Expectations

To provide exceptional service, you need to understand and meet your customers' expectations. Every customer has unique preferences and requirements, so it's essential to be attentive and adaptable. Here are some key aspects to consider:

Quality and Consistency

Customers expect high-quality food with consistent taste and presentation every time they visit your food truck or attend your catering event. This means using fresh ingredients and following standardized recipes. Consistency builds trust and loyalty, as customers know they can rely on you for a great meal every time.

Speed and Efficiency

In the fast-paced world of food trucks and mobile catering, customers appreciate quick and efficient service. Optimize your operations to minimize wait times and streamline the order fulfillment process. Invest in efficient equipment, train your staff to work quickly and accurately, and implement systems to enhance speed and efficiency. This will keep customers happy and coming back for more.

Friendly and Attentive Staff

Your staff is the face of your business. Their interactions with customers can make or break the impression of your food truck or catering service. Hire friendly and personable staff members who are passionate about providing excellent customer service. Train them to be attentive to customer needs, handle complaints professionally, and maintain a positive attitude even during busy times.

Creating Memorable Customer Experiences

Exceptional service goes beyond meeting basic expectations. It's about creating memorable experiences that leave a lasting impression on your customers. Here are some strategies to achieve this:

Personalization

Go the extra mile to make your customers feel special. Get to know their preferences and tailor your service accordingly. Remember their names, favorite dishes, or dietary restrictions, and offer personalized recommendations. Small gestures of personalization can make a big impact and foster customer loyalty.

Engagement and Interactions

Engage with your customers and create a friendly and welcoming atmosphere. Encourage your staff to strike up conversations, ask for feedback, and genuinely connect with customers. Create opportunities for interactions, such as hosting themed events, organizing contests, or offering samples. Building a personal connection with your customers will make them feel valued and increase their satisfaction.

Attention to Detail

Pay attention to the little details that can enhance the overall experience for your customers. Ensure your food truck or catering setup is clean and organized, provide comfortable seating or dining areas, and offer amenities such as hand sanitizers or napkins. Small touches like these demonstrate your dedication to providing a top-notch experience.

Handling Customer Feedback and Complaints

No matter how exceptional your service is, there will be times when you receive feedback or complaints from customers. It's important to handle these situations with professionalism and a willingness to resolve any issues. Here's how to effectively manage customer feedback:

Listen Actively

When a customer provides feedback or raises a complaint, listen attentively and show empathy. Let them express their concerns and frustrations and assure them that their feedback is valued. Active listening shows customers that you care about their experience.

Apologize and Take Responsibility

If something went wrong or if a customer had a negative experience, apologize sincerely and take responsibility for the issue. This demonstrates your commitment to rectifying the situation and provides reassurance to the customer.

Resolve the Issue Promptly

Take immediate action to resolve the problem. Offer solutions, such as replacing the order, providing a refund, or offering a complimentary item. Keep the lines of communication open and ensure that the customer leaves satisfied.

Learn and Improve

Use customer feedback as an opportunity to learn and improve your operations. Analyze common complaints or concerns and identify areas for improvement. Regularly review feedback to make necessary changes and continuously enhance your service.

Conclusion

Providing exceptional service is a key factor in the success of your food truck and mobile catering business. By understanding customer expectations, creating memorable experiences, and effectively handling feedback, you can build a strong reputation and a loyal customer base. Exceptional service not only satisfies customers but also sets you apart from the competition in the industry. Remember, happy customers are your best ambassadors, spreading the word about your delicious food and outstanding service. Keep striving for excellence, and your business will thrive.

Chapter 10: Growing Your Food Truck and Mobile Catering Business

Congratulations on successfully starting your food truck and mobile catering business! You've laid the foundation, and now it's time to shift your focus toward growth and taking your venture to the next level. In this chapter, we'll delve into strategies and tips for expanding your business, increasing your customer base, and exploring new markets.

Expanding Your Menu Offerings

One effective way to grow your food truck and mobile catering business is by expanding your menu offerings. While it's crucial to have a signature dish or specialty that sets you apart, offering a variety of options can attract a wider customer base and keep your existing customers excited and coming back for more.

Start by conducting market research to understand the preferences and dietary needs of your target market. Explore new cuisines, flavors, and dishes that align with your brand and cater to the tastes and trends of your customers. Introducing seasonal specials or limited-time menu items can create a buzz and encourage repeat business.

When expanding your menu, ensure that you have the necessary equipment and supplies to prepare and serve the new dishes efficiently. Training your staff or hiring additional personnel might be necessary to maintain the quality and consistency of your food preparation.

Exploring New Markets

Another strategy for growing your food truck and mobile catering business is by exploring new markets. While you may have established a loyal customer base in your current location, expanding to new areas or targeting different events can open up new opportunities for growth.

Research local events, festivals, and markets that align with your target market and brand. Participating in these events not only exposes your business to a new audience but also allows you to showcase your menu and build brand awareness. Consider collaborating with other food truck owners or catering businesses to increase your presence and attract larger crowds.

In addition to events, explore corporate catering opportunities or partnerships with local businesses for office lunches or special events. Developing relationships with event planners, wedding venues, and corporate clients can lead to regular bookings and recurring revenue.

Investing in Marketing and Advertising

Marketing and advertising play a crucial role in growing your food truck and mobile catering business. Utilize both online and offline marketing strategies to reach your target audience and increase your visibility.

Online Marketing Tactics:

- Maintain a professional website showcasing your brand, menu, and contact information.
- Regularly update your social media platforms with engaging content, including behind-the-scenes footage, recipe stories, and interactive polls or contests.
- Collaborate with food bloggers, influencers, and local publications to generate buzz and reach a wider audience.

Offline Marketing Tactics:

- Distribute flyers or brochures in local businesses and attend networking events.
- Partner with complementary businesses for cross-promotion.
- Invest in eye-catching signage and vehicle wraps for your food truck to create a strong brand presence wherever you go.

Collecting and Encouraging Customer Feedback

As you grow your food truck and mobile catering business, collecting and encouraging customer feedback is essential. Feedback provides valuable insights into customer preferences, areas for improvement, and potential opportunities for growth.

Implement a system for collecting feedback, such as comment cards, online surveys, or feedback forms on your website or social media platforms. Encourage customers to leave reviews on popular review websites and respond promptly and professionally to both positive and negative feedback.

Use customer feedback to refine your menu, improve your service, and enhance the overall customer experience. Consider organizing focus groups or offering special promotions to get direct input from your loyal customers.

Scaling Up and Adding New Units

As your food truck and mobile catering business continues to grow, you may consider scaling up and adding new units. This could involve expanding your fleet of food trucks, acquiring a brick-and-mortar restaurant location, or setting up additional mobile catering units.

Before scaling up, conduct a thorough analysis of your current operations, profitability, and customer demand. Ensure that you have the necessary financial resources, staffing capabilities, and operational systems in place to support the expansion. Seek advice from industry experts, attend industry conferences or workshops, and join food truck associations to learn from others who have successfully scaled their businesses.

Develop a detailed plan for the expansion, including securing financing if needed, hiring and training new staff, and determining the logistics and infrastructure required. Remember to maintain the quality and consistency of your food and service as you scale up. Your success will depend on your ability to replicate the unique and memorable experiences that have attracted customers to your business in the first place.

Conclusion

Growing your food truck and mobile catering business is an exciting and challenging journey. By expanding your menu offerings, exploring new markets, investing in marketing and advertising, collecting and encouraging customer feedback, and scaling up strategically, you can take your business to new heights.

Stay true to your brand, maintain the highest standards of quality, and continuously seek ways to improve and innovate. With perseverance, passion, and a clear growth strategy, your food truck and mobile catering business can achieve long-term success and become a beloved culinary destination in your community.

Enjoy the journey, embrace the challenges, and savor the successes that come your way!